Hands on Dad

Hands on Dad

The Man Every Woman Wants And
The Dad Every Child Needs

DR. ANNIE RUTH FRANCIS

authorHOUSE®

AuthorHouse™
1663 Liberty Drive
Bloomington, IN 47403
www.authorhouse.com
Phone: 1 (800) 839-8640

Published by AuthorHouse   11/17/2015

ISBN: 978-1-5049-5899-8 (sc)
ISBN: 978-1-5049-5900-1 (e)

Print information available on the last page.

Scripture quotations marked KJV are from the Holy Bible, King James Version
(Authorized Version). First published in 1611. Quoted from the KJV Classic
Reference Bible, Copyright © 1983 by The Zondervan Corporation.

Contents

Introduction

This is intended to be a brief and concise message to all fathers and those fathers-to-be. It is my utmost desire that every male will read this book and realize his "God given responsibility," Fatherhood.

It doesn't matter what situation you find yourself in; you can still be a father to your children. Situations may change but fathers don't. Children cannot wait to be loved and nurtured, because every day is important in their lives.

For several years I have had a burning desire to tell every father that he should take an active role in his child's life. If everyone does his part, then we will see a difference in our children. Fathers are just as important in a child's life as mothers.

It is never too late in one's life to learn about the goodness of God. Infants should be sang to and talked to about Jesus. These special times should continue for life wherein everyone will spend some quiet time with God each day.

If children are taught about God and his promises to them then I really think that we would have better children and marriages and thereby making a better world. Today, children are allowed to flaunter around searching for self instead of seeking God. They have society's permission and are said that he or she needs to find them-selves.

Since prayer has been taken out of schools, some children never hear about God. Schools are the only place we can expose every child to the teaching of God since many families do not attend church. Church is a place where everyone can feel that he/she is special and has something to offer society.

There is a big difference in children who attend church and children who don't. The children who attend church exhibit a "satisfaction with self" appearance. I know who I am and where I want to go in life. They respect themselves and others. These children, whether raised in single parent homes or not, have knowledge of their heavenly father and realize that he is supreme and can replace their earthly father or mother.

Learning the true meaning of the Lord's Prayers at an early age makes living beautiful, joyous and prosperous. "Our father, who art in heaven", really means "Our Father," yours and mine who cares about your wellbeing and mine. He is the only one capable of loving and caring for everyone at the same time.

In the book of James S. Schaller, "The Search for Lost Fathering", we learned the importance of the father's role in a child's life. To a small child his father is mighty indeed. When my nephew was a toddler his daddy was everything to him. Whenever it came time for him to eat, take a bath, or go to bed and etc., he would always ask, "my daddy too?' One of my sons favored his daddy so much, until he would get his diaper from me and take it to his father so he could change him. Right now, my grandsons would rather be with their father than their mother or anyone else.

As I was growing up my father was my absolute favorite person in the whole world. It is amazing how well I remember most of our conversations. My father was a Deacon of the church so he was always telling us about Jesus and how wonderful he was and how very much he loved us.

It is something special about a father's presence. Children often feel safe and secure when Dad is around. Most small kids think that dads can handle anything and everything.

Genesis 17:7&8 states, "and I will establish my covenant between me and you and your descendants after you in their generations, for an everlasting covenant, to be God to you and your descendants after you." "Also, I give to you and your descendants after you the land in which you are a stranger, all the land of Canaan, as an everlasting possession; and I will be their God."

My father did everything for his children. He and my mother separated when I was two years old and all six of the children stayed home with dad. Mom moved out, but neither child would leave daddy. So my daddy worked, farmed, trained and raised us in the fear and love of God. I am almost sure that it wasn't easy, but he always seemed to enjoy being around his children.

When he got married again and we, the two younger children went to spend the weekend with our stepmother, we never returned. We were no trouble at all to her. She was loving and kind to us and we showed that we were thankful for her and our newfound home. My father always reminded us of Ephesians 6:14: "Children obey your parents in the Lord: for this is right. Honor thy father and mother, which is the first commandment with promise; that it may be well with thee and thou mayest live on earth. And, ye fathers provoke not your children to wrath: but bring them up in the nurture and admiration of the Lord."

I do believe that my father had a divine intervention and consulted the Lord in everything he did. He nurtured and disciplined his children with love, he never spared the rod, he set rules and penalties, and awards, he would sit us down and explain and encourage us to be the very best that we could. My father certainly stood the test of time and did as James 1:2-4&12 stated: "Consider it pure joy, my brothers, whenever you face trials of many kinds, because you know that the testing of your faith develops perseverance. Perseverance must finish its work so that you may be mature and complete, not lacking anything... Blessed is the man who perseveres under trials, because when he has stood the test, he will receive the crown of life that God has promised to those who love him."

Early Years

The birth of a baby brings much joy to a family. When we look into the face of this beautiful gift from God, What a great feeling it brings to us. Mother, father and grandparents are jubilant and begin planning things for the baby.

As the baby grows, he or she shows that your voice and scent is a comfort. If the baby cries and is picked up by mother or a father he or she usually stops crying. Sometimes when the parent walks into the room, the child shows excitement. You feel so blessed with this child. God blessed you to deposit your seed, now the duty is to take responsibility to nurture, guide and provide this seed that carries your blood in its veins. Do it with pride and enjoy the experience.

At this time we want to give this child the world. Just remember that you are the world to this child. The child is dependent totally upon you to perform your God given responsibility. The child has unconditional love for you. Just be there for the child and do your very best for it. Who knows, you might be raising a president of the United States, a lawyer, a minister or a CPA. This child might end up taking care of you in your latter years.

As the baby grows he or she begins to emulate mom and dad. Often times the little girl will dress up like mommy and the little boy will emulate the father. This is the order of human nature. So we see why it is important for mom and dad to be in the child's life. The little girl will find her way into mom's makeup and put lipstick all over her face. She attempts to color the lips first, but she discovers she has it all over her lips, cheeks and forehead. The little boy will play with toy cars and pretend to drive like daddy. This imitating will continue, even after the child is grown, in a more logical way. If daddy treats mom with respect

1

then the son will treat women with respect. Most girls enjoy helping mom with the house work, especially while they are little. Being in the kitchen is always enjoyable. This is how I learned to cook.[1] I would always station myself in the kitchen with mom while she was cooking. I had never ending questions which she would patiently explain. She would let me break the eggs, whip them and add them to her mixture. It wasn't very long when I could prepare a dish from start to finish with mom looking on. When mom was cleaning greens I would be right there doing little things that she would show me. Each time I got a chance to do more and more until I was allowed to clean them all by myself, but mom was naturally looking on. Today, I clean and cook.

In Rose Werland's article, Custody Disputes, he discussed how the child custody has taken a different twist. Figures from the U.S. Census Bureau showed that in 1995, the latest year available, women had residential custody of children in 85 percent of cases and men in 15 percent. There is a lot those statistics don't explain, such as how many men asked for custody. When men fight for custody, they have a better chance of getting it than the Census figures show." [2]

Middle Years

There is an old Eastern Proverb that states, "If you tell me, I'll forget. If you show me, I may remember. But if you involve me, I'll understand." This Proverb holds true today. As we raise our children we should always keep this in mind. Children learn better when they are involved in activities. Schools now call this, "Hands On". It is a part of most schools curriculum. I learned to cook with this approach. I loved to be in the kitchen while mom was preparing meals. I was full of questions. Mom took the time and answered each one. Gradually, she started letting me chop, stir and break eggs. Next, she showed me how to measure ingredients and add them to mixtures. It wasn't long before I was preparing simple dishes all alone while mom stood by. From small steps to more complicated meals were prepared. At the age of ten I was preparing daily meals for dinner.

Cake baking happened the same way. For years people loved my cakes. One of my sisters would call me when she planned a trip home for me to bake her a sour cream cake. Friends and family members would call and ask, "What did you cook? A lot of times they would drop by just to eat. All of my recipes come from my mom's kitchen. My married son is the main cook at his house and uses some of my recipes. I have enclosed some of my mom's recipes in this book. I sincerely hope that you will use then and involve your child/children in their preparation. I feel certain that the experience will be great and work wonders with your relationship with your kid and together select the recipe to make first.

We all want to save money, especially on food. I have found that fresh vegetables are less expensive at the growers markets or flea markets. I try and go on the last day because items are reduced. The growers don't want to take these vegetables back home to ruin. Check out several grower markets before you choose one. Get acquainted with some of the growers and sometimes they will reduce certain items for you. Always buy green tomatoes and let them get ripe on your counter top slowly. If you need a tomato for a recipe right away, just buy one or two red ones. If you buy green ones you can enjoy tomatoes all week long. Involve your child/children in the shopping experience and the selection process. This will be a lifelong learning experience.

The grower's markets will certainly have a variety of beautiful fresh greens, cabbage squash, peas, okra, sweet potatoes and other food items. Try some of these fresh vegetables and use the recipes from this book. Encourage the kids to eat more fresh vegetables, it's a healthy venture. Introduce your child/children to the growers at the markets, this will send a message to both of them, that you are proud of your child/children.

Let the children help prepare the meal this will entice them to eat some of it. After enjoying the meal, tell the kids that it was delicious and ask them to help with the cleanup. Make a game of the clean-up. You wash and I dry or would you rather dry and I wash? This will be the perfect time to have intense conversations with your child.

Yard work can be done pretty much the same way. Use this as a teaching experience. It would be more fun if you give the child a few dollars afterwards. Show them how you want this job done and next time let them do it alone. We all work harder when there is a reward at the end. Now teach them how to save and manage money. Begin with saving for a movie or a ball game at a specified time. You might need to remind them frequently. The first trip to the movie or ball game, if the child does not have all the money that he needs you might want to make him/her a loan. Explain to him/her that you are expecting the money back at a certain time. Be reasonable; give him time to earn more money. Keep encouraging the child to save money for different events. After the second time, he doesn't have his/her fare; leave him/her at home. Remember this is a training maneuver that is getting your child ready to become a responsible adult. When your child leaves home for college, Military, or some other career, he will know how to clean, cook and manage money.

Each day praise your child. Praise him/her for something he/she has done or for just being your child. We all work harder when we are praised and appreciated. These are some things you can say to your child:

1. I am one lucky guy to have a kid like you.
2. I love you more and more each day.
3. I am so very proud of you.
4. I am proud of the great job you are doing i.e.: *in school, in the chores around the house.*
5. I am excited about how respectful you are.
6. Try and praise your child each day.

Life is a gift from God. What we do with it is our gift to Him.

Florida is among twenty-six states that have switched from favoring custody by one parent to favoring some form of custody or shared custody. Some fathers are taking more of the day-to-day care of their children. Men have begun working from home, reducing their hours at work or even getting jobs with flexible hours so they can spend more quality time with their children.

In my profession as a school counselor, seeing twelve to fifteen year old children especially boys, in need of a fatherly influence shows right through. Mothers can nurture the children, but they cannot teach the boys to be men.

There are many, many fatherless children that need a fatherly word or helping hand from someone. There are numerous reasons why they are fatherless.... death or imprisonment of their fathers & etc. Job 29:16: "I was a father to the poor, and I searched out the case that I did not know." "I, the Lord searched the heart and examine the mind" (Jeremiah 17:10).

Teen Years

As the child approaches the teen years, please pay more attention to him/her. This is the most valuable time of his development. They want to be accepted by their peers. At this age children might do a lot of things adults do not approve of. Your constant attention is required to prevent your child from getting with the wrong crowd or doing something that will cause an undesirable life changing situation. Remember, "It's amazing what a little love can do". I made a practice of cleaning my children's bedrooms once per month without notice. Mattress was turned over, beds were moved, dresser drawers were emptied and cleaned out and the closet was completely cleaned and rearranged. Always beware of what is in your house. Let your child know that privacy is not free. When he/she gets a place of his own, that he pays for then and only then he can have privacy. You have a right to know what's in your house. My advice to you is, "you had better know what's in your house". Yes, I am telling you to snoop. Become a great house detective. Know what's on the child's cell phone, computer and all the pictures sent and received.

Sometimes your child will want to go some places with his/her friends. You volunteer to drive them. This is your opportunity to get to know the friends and their families. Ask questions and get out of the car, go to the door and ask to see the adults in the house. Get telephone numbers and give them yours. This shows that you care about their children and will take care of them while they are in your care. A caring parent will certainly appreciate your concern. Plan an outing with your kid and his/her friends. Have it at a park if you prefer not to entertain them at your house. Put some hot dogs on the grill. Make punch, bottled water potato chips and cookies. Remember to be friendly and have a good time but don't compromise your authorative position. Invite the friend's families so you can get to know more about the friends. Believe me, it will come in handy. Take your camera and take pictures.

Now, let's revisit the snooping that we mentioned. When you drive the kid and friends to the movies or other entertainment activities, park somewhere so you can see the entrance of the place but make sure you are not visible to those coming out of the center. Watch for a while to make sure your charges do not come out and go someplace else. You might be able to trust your kid, but what about the others? Some kids think that they are smarter than the adults and might try and pull a fast one on us from time to time. So keep your antennas up. Try and fill your kid's free time with interesting things and places to go. If we don't provide activities for our kids they will certainly find things to do. "An idle mind is the devil's workshop". This is an old saying that has proven to be very true. Plan trips with the kids; let them find information about the places on the internet. Let them get driving directions, amount of time the trip should take, attractions, restaurants and hotels. Ask them to compare prices of the hotels and then figure out the total cost of the trip for the family. This should prove to be exciting for the kids as well as a great learning experience. If you are taking a rental car let the kids research every car rental company in your city and compare prices and select the most economical one for the family to consider.

We need to provide as many learning situations for our children as possible. Skills learned today will be useful tomorrow, next year and years later. Right now the kids are planning with the family's money but later he will be planning with his own money. This information will be appreciated more at this time. He/She will have the experience of budgeting money and making plans.

I am talking from experience. I raised two boys and later adopted a daughter. My boys and I would sit at the table and pay bills each month. One would read the statements, I would write the check and the other boy was balancing the check book as we went along. Later one would read the statements, the other one would write the checks and I would sign the checks and place them in the envelopes. We would decide on trips for vacation and the boys would visit the library and do the research. We would normally take day trips to amusement parks. Once every two years we would take a trip and spend two or three nights in a hotel. We planned all activities together, Christmas, Birthdays and even church services. So, we know how much money we were going to spend and how much we would save. This carried over to their adult lives.

Please spend time with your children and teach them the good and right things of life. As stated by Quincy Jones, "It's amazing how much trouble you can get into when you don't have anything else to do". Encourage your child to develop a hobby or hobbies, something that doesn't always involve other people. Teach the children that they need to know the people that they keep company with. Some people have gotten into trouble, not because they did anything wrong, but because they were with the wrong people at the wrong time. Years ago while working in health care on the evening shift (3:00 p.m. – 11:00 p.m.) a young man was working there while attending school during the day. He was a very dependable and hardworking young man. He was always on time and always reported to work when on schedule. One day he didn't show up nor called. The staff and supervisor were very concerned about him. We didn't know what had happened, but knew something had to have happen. About three hours later he showed up much shaken. He told us that he was on his way to work when he stopped to pick up a hitch hiker. Right afterwards a policeman pulled him over (reason unknown). They were searched and so was the car. A small amount of marijuana was found between the seats. They were both taken to jail. He explained to the policeman that the drugs were not his and he had never seen the hitch hiker before, but was only giving him a ride. It took two hours for the policeman to get the hitchhiker to confess that he didn't know the young man, but he was nice enough to give him a ride and the drugs were his. He had stuck them between the seats when they were stopped.

When your child begins driving alone, please demand that he/she does not ride a lot of people in the vehicle. He/She will never know what other people have on them. You need to impress upon them how much responsible driving a vehicle carries with it. Teach them to watch as well as pray. Take your child/children to church and Sunday school. They might like to participate in the choir or the usher's board or some other activities at the church. When I was a kid I looked forward to going to church and Sunday school. We got the chance to hold different positions at Sunday school and became comfortable speaking in front of people. This adds to a child's learning experiences that will carry over to school. Most churches have organized activities for children of all ages. There are normally professional, even teachers who work with children at Sunday school and other church activities. These times and activities will give parents the opportunity to get to know the teachers and other professionals that will enhance the children's lives. If your child/children know that you will see their teacher at the church on Sunday, he/she will normally put on his/her best behavior at school. When I was growing up, several teachers from school attended the same church as we did. They knew my family and you bet your bottom dollar, I put on my very best behavior at school. I was no fool; I wanted my teachers to say positive things about me to my parents when they saw them on Sundays. Many professional singers, actors and actresses got their beginning in church.

Attending church activities might help deter children from our juvenile system. Teach them if an officer pulls them over be polite. Always say, "Yes sir/mam, no sir/mam, please and thank you". This kind of responses still will show respect, no matter how old we get. Tell your child to stay in the car until the officer asks him/her to step outside.

The following is a listing of the number of kids in juvenile custody in each state in the U.S. in 1997 and 2007.

	1997	2007
United States	75406	60426
Alabama	1266	1113
Alaska	276	189
Arizona	129	861
Arkansas	507	711
California	13770	8901
Colorado	1023	1329
Connecticut	516	300
Delaware	177	198
D.C.	120	165
Florida	3963	4419
Georgia	2316	1413
Hawaii	108	87
Idaho	171	384
Illinois	2457	1875

Indiana	1830	1902
Iowa	771	759
Kansas	825	759
Kentucky	843	693
Louisiana	2190	849
Maine	225	108
Maryland	909	453
Massachusetts	606	639
Michigan	2604	2085
Minnesota	1167	1029
Mississippi	630	240
Missouri	993	945
Montana	267	159
Nebraska	495	369
Nevada	498	678
New Hampshire	153	135
New jersey	1200	873
New Mexico	594	249
New York	3852	2745
North Carolina	930	831
North Dakota	162	186
Ohio	2970	3021
Oklahoma	519	684
Oregon	1200	1080
Pennsylvania	3120	3618
Rhode Island	360	180
South Carolina	1215	813
South Dakota	390	309
Tennessee	1716	927
Texas	5268	4599
Utah	534	627
Vermont	30	15

Virginia	1662	1341
Washington	1611	1095
West Virginia	192	402
Wisconsin	1572	1149
Wyoming	312	222
Tribal Facilities	0	15
Not Reported	3027	1704

The schools all employ sheriff deputies as resource officers in the schools. Call and speak to one, make an appointment and discuss a way to prevent juvenile delinquency. They have several programs in place already. They are there to help and seem to take pride in their work. They are there to prevent kids from entering the juvenile justice system. New laws and statues are reported in the local newspaper each year. Read and discuss them with your child/children.

During election times, look at each candidate and encourage your child/children to research each one and discuss them with the family. When the child turns eighteen and registers to vote he/she will know how to become an informed voter. Encourage him/her to be an informed citizen and stay alert about things going on around him/her; new streets, new stores, new buildings and etc.

Don't forget, occasionally, ask your child/children what career choice is appealing to them. They might change sometimes. Ask them what kind of house they would like to live in and what kind of car they want to drive? Then ask them to research each career. Tell them to find out what kinds of courses it requires, how much it pays and what parts of the country the jobs are most likely in. Now remember you are getting them ready to be out on their own.

You need to teach them how to prepare simple meals, wash clothes, iron and get around on public transportation. If they go away to school or move into their own place, these skills will certainly pay off. When I was in college I overheard a conversation between a young man and a young lady. The young man was in an unhappy marriage. The young lady asked him, "Why did you get married?" He replied, "I married so I could have someone to cook for me." Please teach your daughters and your sons to cook. My mom taught my brother and me to cook. I also taught my two sons to cook. Each one prepared planned meals for a month. I was always accessible if they needed me. These are life skills. They will not have all their meals from McDonalds or Burger King.

Now your child/children are ready for adulthood. When they leave home you may not have to worry, because you have prepared them to take care of themselves. Keep in touch with them and guide them whenever they need help. Remember, always encourage them and let them know that you are proud of them.

Your child/children are approaching young adulthood. It is time to sit down and have that manly talk with them. I trust that you have been talking to them all along about the "birds and the bees". Now it is time to call it what is, "sex". Let them know to be very selective in choosing a friend. Tell them that they are responsible for their actions. I would have the doctor talk with him/her. The health department is an excellent source of information. The health nurse will talk in terms that children can understand. You can get in touch with the nurse through the school or health department in your area. Use the resources that are available to you. This is why they are here.

Society has in previous years nurtured girls more than boys and somewhat left boys to pretty much find their own way and excused their behavior by saying "Boys will be boys." This has proven to be most harmful to our society. There is more violence in schools today than ever before, and more children in trouble, in the Juvenile Justice system and doing time.

Romans 4:23&24: "Now it was not written for his sake alone that it was imputed to him." "But also for us, it shall be imputed to us who believe in him who raised up Jesus our Lord from the dead."

Our sins separate us from God; not doing right is a sin. When we bring children into this world they are our God given responsibility. We should nurture and love them according to God's commandments. As stated in Psalm 127:3 children are a heritage from the Lord." Matthew 17:6 "But whoever causes one of these little one who believe in me to sin, it would be better for him if a millstone were hung around his neck, and he were drowned in the depth of the sea." Proverb 20:11 even a child is known by his deeds, whether what he does is pure and right."

Children are very important to Jesus as stated in Matthew 18:1-4 "At the time the disciples came to Jesus, saying, "Who then is greatest in the kingdom of heaven/" "Then Jesus called a little child to him, set him in the midst of them and said, "Assuredly, I say to you, unless you are converted and become as little children, you will by no means enter the kingdom of heaven." "Therefore whoever humbles himself as this little child is the greatest in the kingdom of heaven."

Some psychologists believe that boys are more fragile than girls, so now we should redirect our focus. Men are more reluctant to discuss their health issues and some men refuse to seek routine medical care. I tend to agree with a story by Will Courneay, an expert on men's health, that men die seven years younger than women partly because of attitudes and behaviors associated with a "boys will be boys" society.

When society starts respecting the family's true foundation that everything is based upon, we will enjoy a more pleasant loving world in which to live. God has already established the family's role.

In "Boys are at a higher risk" by Ovetta Sampson, The Tallahassee Democrat, Tuesday, May 16, 2000, If one takes responsibility for his relationship with God it will truly impact his marriage, children, neighbors and others. When God makes a covenant with man, it usually includes his descendants as well. Our faith in God is the most important thing that we can pass on to our children.

We should forever be mindful that the way we live is not just for our personal life only but for our seed. This so stated in Isaiah 59:21: "As for me, "says the Lord, "this is my covenant with them; My spirit who is upon you and my words which I have put in your mouth shall not depart from your mouth, nor from the mouth of your descendants, nor from the mouth of your descendants' descendants says the Lord, "From this time and forevermore." For this reason I talk with my children constantly about the love of Jesus Christ and encourage them to be in touch with him. My life, hopefully, is a testimony of our living Christ. I want everyone, not just my children and grandchildren to see God in my life as I talk with them and walk among them. I pray that my off springs will put their trust in God and will not forget his deeds and keep his commandments. As I pass my faith down to them as my father did for me, then I pray that my children will pass it down to their children and so on. This is so emphasized in Psalms 78:2-7: "I will utter hidden things from old. What we have heard and known what our fathers have told us. We will not hide them from their children; we will tell the next generation the praiseworthy deeds of the Lord his power, and the wonders he has done. He decreed his statutes for Jacob and established the law in Israel, which he commanded our forefathers to teach their children, so the next generation would know them, even the children yet to be born, and they in turn would tell their children. Then they would put their trust in God and would not forget his deeds but will keep his commandments."

As stated in Paul Meier and Richard Meier's family foundations: "Some foundations for spiritual development are laid during infancy." The child can sense the overall home atmosphere, and will begin to respond to the parents' behavior and attitudes. A child's perspective of God will depend largely upon what his earthly father is like. The child will develop a basic trust that will enable him later to have a meaningful faith in God if he is provided with a loving secure and accepting environment.[2] Attending Sunday School and worship service regularly as a family will strengthen our family unit.

"The church can meet the needs, both spiritual and emotional, of its members. The church can provide "fathering", "mothering", "brothering" and "sistering" in a way that makes up for deficiencies of childhood."

We need to remember always that God's main purpose is to reconcile a lost world to him. He works from his kingdom perspective with eternity in mind. Every person needs to do his part and walk by faith, and not sight. Let us not become weary in doing (good), for at the proper time we will reap a harvest if we do not give up (Galatians 6:9).

Later Years

When the children leave home for school you will get the opportunity to do some things that you would like to do without rushing back home. You might want to take a two week vacation. Whatever you do make sure your children can get in touch with you. You can't give up yet. Remember, once a parent always a parent. It's not hands on but verbal reassurance from time to time. Make sure you continue to make as much money as possible because most of your calls from the children will be for you to send money. Each time you should remind them to manage their time and money wisely.

In four or five years, your child will be going into the real word, "work". She/he will be in control of his life. It might not be very long before he wants to get married. Please meet his young lady and her parents. Remember, a good relationship with the in-laws and family will prove to be important. You and the other family will share grandchildren. Grandchildren are the biggest blessing that one can get. Remember how excited you were when your first child was born? Multiply that same feeling by ten. It is exciting to hold and cuddle this child. Whenever the child smiles, it will certainly warm your heart. You will impatiently wait for the next smile. Each milestone the child reaches will be an occasion to celebrate.

It is my belief that every child would like to think of his earthly father as we do our heavenly father, as a guardian and a guide. Children want to be assured that their father will always be there for them.

Fathers, my plea to you is, please take your fatherly responsibility seriously and enjoy the experience. Whenever you plan to do the right thing, God will place helpers all along your path to assist you in times of need. Therefore, take no thought, saying what shall we eat? Or what shall we drink? Or wherewithal shall we be clothed? For your heavenly father knoweth that ye have need of all these things," (Matthew 6:31&32)

Selected Bibliography

1. <u>The Holy Bible</u>
   New King James Version

2. The Tallahassee Democrat
   Ross Werland "Custody Disputes", Tuesday, May 2, 2000 and Ovetta Sampson "Boys are at a higher risk", Tuesday, May 16, 2000

3. <u>Family Foundation</u>
   How to have a happy home, Paul Meier and Richard Meier, Fifth Printing 1995

4. <u>The Man God Uses</u>
   Henry and Tom Blackaby, 1998

5. The Number of Juveniles in Committed Custody in The United States- 1997 and 2007 Sickmund, Melissa, Sldky, T.J., and Kang Wei. (2011) "Census of Juveniles in Residential Placement Datebook"

About the Author

I have had the good pleasure of knowing Dr. Annie Ruth Francis for more than two decades, and she has always portrayed noteworthy qualities of spiritual virtues, of womanhood and uplift.

Dr. Francis is an exemplary parent, teacher, counselor and a role model for young adults. I am pleased that she has chosen to pen her wealth of knowledge and experiences to share with us during such a time as these.

Less than thirty percent of black families have a dad in the household. Dr. Francis' book: *Hands on Dad* addresses this problem and offer meaningful solutions and consequences of societal problems. Parents, teachers and young adults should have a copy of this book as a guiding principle for parents and for those waiting in the balance. *Hands on Dad* can serve to retard and finally alleviate the catastrophic of teenage pregnancy, the high rate of black boys dropping out of high school and the use and sale of drugs and filling our jails and prisons.

Young boys and girls who read *Hands on Dad* will recapture the vital role of fatherhood in the family and take marriage more seriously as the cornerstone to a meaningful and lasting society.

Dr. Ossifield Anderson, PH.D.

My name is Dorothy Caswell; I am a retired Speech Therapist for Leon County Schools in Tallahassee, Florida. Annie Ruth Francis is a dear friend and colleague of mine.

I first met Annie Ruth in 1979 when I was hired as a Speech Therapist at a school for exceptional (handicapped) students, where she held the position of guidance counselor/nurse. She did social work, meeting the students' needs through coordination with their parents, families, teachers and the community at large. She was very competent and proficient in her job as nurse/counselor. The skill, knowledge, cares and compassion she demonstrated with these students and their parents was remarkable.

Of course, Ruth is just as caring with her own children. As a single mother of two sons I marveled at the love devotion, dedications, and guidance she gave to them in all their endeavors, somehow she found the time. I, being single too and the mother of two daughters learned so much from her.

In the years that I've known her, some things I know for sure: She is a solid Christian. She is grounded in her faith. She is always involved in her church. She loves to read, cook and go fishing, but it is when she doing something with or for children that she is most fulfilled.

Dorothy Caswell

Dedication

This book is dedicated to my son, Renard Head, who is an exemplary father to his sons, Justin and Devin, and to the memory of my deceased son, Demone Head, who was wise beyond his years and truly loved the Lord with all of his heart. He excelled in everything he undertook, because he always put God first. He would often tell me that before I do anything, I should take it through heaven first.

I am also dedicating this book to my brother, Nathaniel Maxwell who so graciously stood in the gap as father to my sons due to their absent daddy, I am forever grateful to him. This, I am certain, helped Renard to become the great father that he is today and to my brother James, who always took time to interact with all the children of the Maxwell clan.

I sincerely thank God for giving me a God fearing father who passed his love of God down to his children and they in turn passed it to their children. Today I am a proud mother and grandmother who are constantly thanking God for his many, many blessings in my life.

Galatians 3:20: and if you are Christ's, then you are Abraham's seed, and heirs according to the promise. My life is a true testimony of the promise of God.

Dedicated also to my adoptive daughter, TyTy who has been a pure joy to raise. Glory be to God for all his many, many blessings in my life.

Vegetables

Salad

1 head lettuce
2 tomatoes
½ sweet onions
½ green bell pepper
½ red peppers
1/8 cup shredded carrots

Directions

Cut lettuce into small pieces use colander: and wash lettuce under running cold water. Drain, wrap lettuce in paper towels and place in freezer. Chop onion, green and red peppers. Mix in bowl, add shredded carrots. Chop tomatoes and place in a separate bowl. Add lettuce and toss well. Serve and put tomato on each servicing.

Broccoli Salad

1 cup broccoli florets
1/8 cup raisins
¼ cup chopped sweet
onions
½ cup croutons
Olive oil

Directions
Wash florets; mix in bowl with raisins, chopped onions and croutons.
Sprinkle with olive oil. Toss well and serve.

Dr. Annie Ruth Francis

Onion, Cucumber and Tomato Salad

2 to 3 cucumbers
½ sweet onions
2 small tomatoes
Olive oil
Vinegar

Directions

Wash Cucumber well, cut them into thin slices; slice onions in very thin slices also slice tomatoes into thin slices. Mix in bowl, sprinkle with olive and small amount of vinegar. Cool for 20 minutes and serve.

French Fried Eggplant

Small Firm eggplant
Oil
Salt
Pepper

Directions
Wash eggplant. Peel eggplant. Cut in half (the long way). Take the seeds out. Cut into French fries wash under running water, drain on paper towels. Salt and pepper to taste. Place eggplant fries into hot oil, cook until brown and remove from oil and drain on clean paper towels.

Scallion Eggplant

1 medium eggplant-peeled and sliced ½ in. thick
½ cup salad oil
¼ cup tomato sauce (from
¼ cup grated cheese
1 teaspoon o- salt and pepper
3 large tomatoes- peeled and cut into ½ in. slices
3 slices mozzarella cheese

Directions
Brown eggplant in salad oil- Drain on paper towel- mix tomato sauce, grated cheese, oregano, salt and pepper in a 1 cup measure. Make 2 layers each of eggplant a tomato slice with tomato sauce mixture divided evenly between. Bake uncovered in 350 degree oven for 30 minutes- Place mozzarella on top and bake 10-15 min. more.

Dried Lima Beans

1 pack of dried lima beans
Meat for seasoning (pork, smoked turkey parts)
Salt
Pepper

Directions
Wash beans, place in a pot of water with meat for seasoning, boil on high for 5 minutes, and reduce heat to medium, cook for 30 min. Add salt and pepper; reduce heat to low and cook until beans are very tender and water is cook down and thick.

Black-eyed Peas

1 Pack black-eyed peas
Meat for seasoning) pork, smoked turkey parts)
Salt
Pepper

Directions
Wash peas, place in a pot of water with meat boil for 5 to 10 min. on high. Reduce heat and salt and pepper. Cook on low, heat for 1 ½ hrs. or until peas are tender and juice is low and thick. Remove from heat.

Spinach

1 pack of baby spinach
Salt butter or margarine
½ onions

Directions
Wash spinach, removing stems. Sauté sliced onion in butter or margarine. Place spinach in the pan over the onion. Salt to taste, let cook, turning once or twice for 15 minutes on medium.

Dr. Annie Ruth Francis

Mustard Green Soup

Small amount of mustard greens
Self-rising meal ½ cups
Salt Pepper
Bacon
1 small hot pepper
Wash greens thoroughly, cut into small pieces, cook bacon in a pot and the greens, and cook covered for 7 to 8 min. Add hot chopped pepper, salt and pepper. Add ½ cup water and cook on low. Mix meal with water, make sure it is stiff. Roll into small balls. Place balls into pot and continue to cook for another 20 min.

<u>Tomatoes and Rice</u>

1 cup cooked rice
2 slice of bacon
2 or 3 ripe tomatoes
1 small can tomato sauce
Salt
Pepper
1 onion
1 rib celery
½ bell pepper

<u>Directions</u>
Cook bacon in a deep pot, add chopped tomatoes, onion, celery, bell pepper. Cook for 15 min. Add cooked rice, salt and pepper. Cook for another 30 minutes. Cool and serve.

Potato Soup

2 or 3 large white potatoes
2 tablespoons butter
Salt
Pepper
½ chopped onion (if desired)

Directions
Peel potatoes, chop in small pieces. Place in pot with 2 ½ cups water, bring to a boil, and add onion, salt, pepper and butter. Cook on medium heat until water is low and thick. Cool and serve.

Collard Soup

1 small bunch collard greens
4 slices bacon
3 tablespoons melted butter
½ cup chopped onion
1 green pepper, sliced
1 chicken bouillon cube
1 cup boiling water
Half and half or milk
Salt pepper

Direction

Wash Collard leaves, cut into small ribbons. Fry bacon in deep pot, add chopped onions, green pepper, stir until for three minutes, add water, bouillon cube and cook collards for 20 minutes. Add half and half or milk, salt, pepper and melted butter. Cook on low for 1 hour or until tender.

<u>Collard Greens</u>

Collards
Seasoning meat (ham hocks or smoked turkey parts)

Directions
Cut green leaves away from the stacks. Cut leaves into small pieces. Wash thoroughly until well cleaned. Place greens into pot, cover with water and place seasoning meat into pot with greens. Bring to a boil, reduce heat and cook covered for 45 minutes to 1 ½ hrs. until tender. Salt to taste and you may use a piece of hot pepper if desired.

Mustard Greens

Green leaves
Bacon
Salt
Green pepper

Directions
Clean the green leave thoroughly. Brown bacon in the pot. Place cleaned greens on top of bacon with the dripping, put a top on the pot and let cook on medium heat, checking greens often. Mustards provide their own water. Season to taste and cook for 30 minutes or more until tender.

<u>Turnips</u>

Green leaves
Bacon
Hot green pepper

<u>Directions</u>
Cook turnips the same way mustards were cooked. Make sure they are cleaned thoroughly

<u>Cabbage</u>

Salt
Pepper
Hot green pepper

<u>Directions</u>
Cut cabbage into wedges or small pieces. Wash thoroughly. Place seasoning into hot pot. Place washed greens into pot with seasoning. Cook for 10 to 15 min. on medium heat.

<u>Yellow Squash</u>

4 to 5 medium yellow squash
1 small onion
Butter or margarine 4 tablespoons
Salt
Pepper
Onion

<u>Directions</u>
Wash the squash thoroughly. Cut into small pieces. Cut onion slices. Place margarine (butter) into frying pan. Place onion and squash into pan. Cook about 5 minutes with top on. Stir occasional and remove from heat, season to taste.

Brussels sprouts

Brussels sprouts
Margarine (Butter) or oil
Salt
Pepper

Directions
Cut in half. Heat small amount of oil or margarine. Place sprouts in pan. Cook on medium heat while turning sprouts about 5 min. Reduce heat, season to taste. Cook for another 2 min.

Broccoli

Broccoli
Salt
Pepper
Cheese

Directions
Cut stalks away from broccoli. Wash thoroughly. Place broccoli in a pot with a very small amount of water for steaming. Season to taste. Steam from 3 to 5 minutes. Melt a slice of cheese on the servings for kids (this is a smart way to get kids to eat broccoli) they will love you for this.

<u>Macaroni and Cheese</u>

Elbow Mac ½ small box
Flour 2 tablespoons
Milk 1 ½ to 2 cups
Cheese- Velveeta cheese makes a creamy sauce

<u>Directions</u>
Cook macaroni according to directions on package. Make cheese sauce by mixing milk, flour and cheese in a double boiler over low heat. Salt and pepper to taste. Put macaroni in a baking dish and pour the cheese sauce over it, bake for 18 to 20 min.

Mashed Potatoes

3 to 4 white potatoes
Butter
Milk ½ cup
Salt
Pepper

Directions

Cut potatoes into small pieces and boil until very tender. Mash potatoes- making sure no lumps remain. Put two tablespoons of butter in potatoes. Use milk to thin potatoes. Salt and pepper to taste.

Left over Baked Sweet Potatoes

Baked Potatoes
Oil

Directions

Peel the potatoes. Slice potatoes thinly. Put a small amount of oil in skillet. Heat the oil. Place sliced potatoes into skillet brown potatoes on each side. Drain on paper towels.

Cauliflower

Cauliflower
Oil
Salt
Pepper
Margarine

Directions
Wash cauliflower well. Place in a pot with small amount of water for steaming. Season with salt, pepper and margarine. Steam cauliflower for 5 to 6 minutes

Fried Rice with Vegetables

1 cup cooked rice
4 tablespoons oil
1 small onion chopped finely
½ bell pepper chopped finely
1 rib celery chopped finely
1 small hot pepper if desired

Directions

Stir fry onion, bell peppers, celery and hot pepper in skillet with 2 tablespoons. Oil for 3 min. Remove vegetables and set aside. Stir fry rice in remaining oil. Combine the vegetables with rice; stir fry for 3 minutes or more.

Eggplant with Tomato Sauce

1 medium eggplant-peeled and sliced
½ cup oil
¼ cup tomato sauce
¼ grated cheese of choice
1 tablespoon oregano
Salt and Pepper to taste
3 large tomatoes sliced
3-4 slices of mozzarella cheese

Directions

Brown eggplant in oil. Drain on paper towel. Combine tomato sauce, grated cheese, oregano, salt and pepper. Layer eggplant, tomato slices in a cooking dish. Pour sauce over layer. Cook for 25 to 30 min. Place mozzarella cheese slices on top and bake another 10 min.

<u>Linguine Salad</u>

1 package of linguine
4 tomatoes chopped
3 cucumbers chopped
1 bunch of spring onions chopped
½ small red onions chopped
½ yellow and ½ green peppers
3 small chopped carrots
1 to 2 pounds of shrimp
2 tablespoons of McCormick vegetable supreme seasoning
1 bottle of Zesty Italian dressing

<u>Directions</u>
Cook linguine according to package directions. Combine the chopped items in a large bowl with linguine. Steam peeled cleaned and chopped shrimp. Combine with mixture. Pour the entire bottle of zesty Italian salad dressing over the mixture and stir well. Place in refrigerator until serving time.

Dr. Annie Ruth Francis

Pound Cake

4 cups sugar
2 sticks unsalted butter
8 eggs
1 tsp. soda
½ tsp. salt
1 tsp. baking soda
1tsp vanilla
4 ½ cups flour
2 cups buttermilk

Directions

Cream sugar and butter sift together flour, salt, soda and baking powder. Beat well. Add eggs (one at a time) alternating with part flour and part buttermilk. Mix well. Pour mixture into a greased and lightly floured pan. Bake for 1 ½ hours at 350°. Remove from oven, place on damp paper towel and let cool. Run a flat knife around edges of cake. Flip cake over on a cake plate after it cools.

Sour Cream Pound Cake

1 tsp. soda
½ lb. butter
3 cups sugar
6 eggs tsp. vanilla ½ pt. sour cream 3 cups shifted cake flour

Directions
Cream butter and sugar together. Add eggs alternating with flour beating well after each. Add sour cream and vanilla beating well. Pour mixture in a greased and lightly floured tub pan. Bake 1 ½ hours on 350° degrees.

Green Beans

Fresh green beans or string beans
Bacon or margarine
Salt
Pepper
Bay leaf

Directions

Wash beans well. Cut ends from beans. Place beans in pot with fried bacon or margarine. Salt and pepper to taste. Place one bay leaf in pot and cook on medium heat. Cook for 15 min. so beans stay firm.

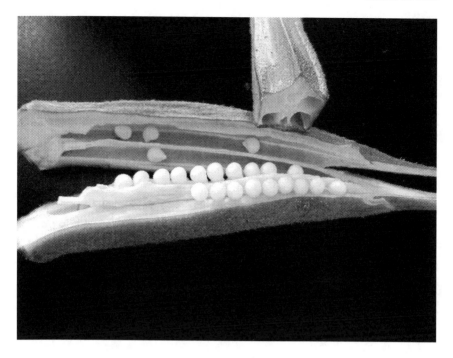

Fried Okra

Select small tender pods of okra
Oil
Salt
Pepper

Directions

Wash okra, drain on paper towel. Cut into small pieces. Place a small amount of oil in frying pan, just enough to coat the pan. Place okra into pan, Salt and pepper to taste. Cook over medium heat for 5 min. turning over with a spatula. Reduce heat and place top on pan, turning often to prevent burning and sticking. Cook for 15 to 20 min.

Fried Green Tomatoes

Firm green tomatoes
Oil
Salt
Pepper
One egg (if desired)

Directions

Wash tomatoes. Place on paper towel. Slice tomatoes into medium slices. Salt and pepper to taste. Beat egg in well and mix two tablespoons of milk or water with egg. Dredge tomato slices in egg then in the flour, sake excess flour from tomato slices. Place tomato slices in hot oil. Brown on each side over medium heat. Remove from oil and drain on clean paper towels.

Fried Yellow Squash

Squash (yellow preferred)

Oil
Salt
Pepper
Egg if desired

Directions
Wash and slice squash. Salt and pepper to taste. If egg used, follow the green tomato recipe.

Lima Beans

1 package of lima beans
1 or 2 ham hocks or 2 to 3 smoked turkey wings
Salt
Pepper

Directions
Wash beans; place them in a pot with water that covers the beans. Place ham hocks or smoked turkey wings (pre-washed) into the pot. Cook on high until it begins to boil, reduce heat to medium and cook for 30 min. Then reduce heat to low and cook for 1 hour. Salt and pepper to taste.

Squash Casserole

Squash- 5 small
2 eggs
Butter 2 tablespoons
Salt
Pepper
Flour 2 tablespoons
Cheese

Directions
Wash squash, drain on a paper towel. Melt butter; pour in the eggs and flour. Steam squash in 1 cup water. Blend squash in blender and egg mixture, salt and pepper and blend 2 minutes more. Mixture should not be thin or soupy. Add more flour if needed. Bake until firm. Add cheese on top about 5 min. before removing from oven.

Squash Pie

5 small yellow squash
1 cup butter
1 cup sugar
1 tablespoon vanilla flavor
1 egg
5 tablespoon corn starch
1 pie crust

Directions

Wash squash, cut in small pieces and boil in ¼ cup water until very tender, drain, blend until very fine. Mix with sugar, butter, egg, corn starch and flavor. Pour mixture browned pie crust, bake with cheese slices on top until done.

Corn Bread

1 cup self-rising meal
2 tablespoons sugar
½ cup milk
¼ cup oil
1 egg

Directions
Put meal into a deep bowl, add sugar, stir in milk, stir in the egg. Add the oil and stir well. Oil the baking pan and pour batter into pan. Bake at 350 degrees until done and brown on top. Remove from oven.

Corn Bread with Corn

1 cup self rising meal
2 tablespoons of sugar
½ cup milk
¼ cup oil
1 egg
¼ cup corn kernels

Directions

Put meal into a deep bowl, add sugar, stir in milk, stir in the egg. Add the oil and stir well. Oil the baking pan and pour batter into pan. Bake at 350 degrees until done and brown on top. Remove from oven.

Corn Bread Muffins

1 cup self-rising meal
1 egg
¼ cup oil 2 tablespoons sugar
½ cup milk

Directions
Mix all ingredients in a deep bowl. Pour mixture into greased muffin tins. Bake for 30 minutes at 350 degrees. Remove from oven and place the baking tin on a damp paper towel for 3 minutes. Remove each muffing from the tins.

Crackling Corn Bread

1 cup self-rising corn meal
1 egg
2 tablespoons sugar
½ cup milk
2 tablespoons oil
¼ cup pork cracklings

Directions
Mix meal and sugar with milk and stir in egg. Mix well. Stir in oil and cracklings. Mix well. Bake in a greased baking pan for 30 minutes on 350 degrees. Remove from oven and cool before cutting.

Corn Bread Patties

1 cup self-rising meal
½ cup milk
2 tablespoons sugar
¼ cup oil
1 egg

Directions

Mix meal, milk, sugar, egg and oil in a mixing bowl. Heat a frying pan (iron skillet preferable) on the stove. Oil the bottom of pan; pour a small amount of batter in 2 or 3 sections of the skillet. Cook on low heat; turn over in about 5 to 6 seconds. Cook until brown on each side. Repeat until all batter is cooked.

Meats
Pot Roast

Onion- small chopped
Garlic (1 clove) chopped
½ bell pepper (if desired) chopped
1 rib celery chopped
Salt
Pepper
3 tablespoons flour

Directions
Wash meat under running water. Place on paper towels. Brown onion, garlic, bell pepper and celery in oil. Set aside. Brown meat on each side in same container. Remove meat, brown flour and ½ cup water and return meat and browned vegetables to the meat. Cook on medium heat for 15 min. Reduce heat. Salt and pepper and continue to cook until tender. Serve with rice or mashed potatoes.

Boston Butt Roast

Roast
Onion chopped
Celery chopped
Garlic chopped
Salt
Pepper
1/3 cup water

Directions
Place washed roast in a deep roasting pan. Salt and pepper. Place onion, celery and garlic in pan around meat. Pour water in pan and cover cooking on 350 degrees for 1 hour or until tender.

Dr. Annie Ruth Francis

Smothered Pork Chops

Pork chops (bone in)
Flour 3 tablespoons
Salt pepper
Onion chopped
1 tablespoon oil
¼ cup water

Directions
Wash pork chops Salt and pepper on each side. Dredge in flour on each side. Brown chops in oil. Remove and brown flour in the remaining oil. Pour in water and stir. Return chops and onions to pan. cover, reduce heat and cook covered for 5 to 8 min.

Oven Fried Chicken

Chicken parts
Corn flakes-crushed fine in blender
Salt
Pepper
Poultry
Seasoning
Cooking spray
Egg

Directions
Wash chicken, drain on paper towels. Blended corn flakes, add seasoning to corn flakes. Beat egg in a deep bowl and a little water or milt to the beaten egg. Dip chicken in egg wash. Place dipped chicken in corn flakes (cover well). Spray baking pan and place chicken on pan. Bake for 20 to 30 minutes, turn over and cook for another 20 min. on 350 degrees.

Dr. Annie Ruth Francis

Broiled Chicken

Chicken parts
Cooking spray
Salt
Pepper
Poultry seasoning

Directions
Wash chicken drain on paper towel. Season with salt, pepper and poultry season. Spray cooking pan with cooking spray. Place chicken on pan and bake for 30 min. at 350 degrees. Turnover and continue baking or 20 min.

Fried Chicken

Chicken parts
Salt
Pepper
Poultry seasoning
Oil
Flour

Directions
Wash chicken, removing as much fat as possible. Place washed chicken on clean paper towels to dry. Season chicken on both sides. Coat chicken in flour, shake excess flour from chicken. Place chicken in hot oil. Cook on medium heat, turning when necessary. Make sure chicken is well done. Remove chicken from oil, draining it on paper towels.

Turkey Wings

Turkey wings
Salt
Pepper
Poultry seasoning
Onion
Garlic clove
Bay leaf

Directions
Wash wings. Place in a baking pan or pot for boiling. Salt and pepper to taste. Cut onion and place over wings. Place garlic and bay leaf over wings. Cover and cook over medium heat for 1 ½ hours

Roasted Chicken

1 whole chicken
Salt
Pepper
2 tablespoons oil
Poultry seasoning
½ lemons

Directions

Wash chicken well then rub the oil over chicken put poultry seasoning on all sides. Squeeze the juice from the ½ lemon, sprinkle over the chicken. Cover with foil paper. Place in oven at 350 degrees for 1 ½ hours with 1/8 cup water in a pan underneath the chicken.

Dr. Annie Ruth Francis

Grill Chicken

Chicken parts
1/8 cup oil
½ cup salt
½ cup sugar
Pepper
Poultry seasoning
Coals
Seasoned wood

Directions

Wash chicken, pat dry and make a solution of water with ½ cup salt and ½ cup sugar. Place chicken in the solution for 15 to 20 min. Remove chicken and pat dry. Brush chicken parts with oil and season with salt pepper and poultry seasoning. Heat grill with hot coals. Place seasoned wood on top of coals. Place a pan of water on one side of grill. Place chicken parts on grill. Put the grill top down, let cook for 1 hour with skin side up. Check chicken and turn over. Cook for 30 minutes more. Remove from grill and enjoy.

Chicken and Rice

1 cup rice
4 chicken breast
1 onion
Salt
Pepper
Poultry seasoning
1 rib celery
½ bell pepper

Directions
Boil chicken. Cool and debone, discarding bones place chicken chopped onion, celery and bell pepper and rice in a pot with 2 ½ cups of reserved liquid, cook on medium for 15 minutes, reducing heat to low season with salt, pepper and poultry season. Cook until rice is done.

Pan Broiled Fish

Fish

Directions
Wash fish, pat dry with paper towel, heat oil in (just enough oil in bottom of frying pan), salt and pepper each side of fish. Place fish in hot pan reducing heat to medium. Cook on each side turning over with spatula. Cook until fork tender and well done.

<u>Hog Maws</u>

1 pack hog maws
1 onion
1 clove garlic
Salt
Pepper

<u>Directions</u>

Cut maws into small pieces, wash and place into a pot with water covering meat. Add chopped onion and garlic. Boil on high for 15 to 20 min. Reduce heat to low, add salt and pepper, continue to cook for 1 ½ hours or until meat is fork tender and liquid is very low and thick. Serve over rice

<u>Quail</u>

6 quails
1 onion
1 cup oil
Salt
Pepper
Poultry seasoning
½ cup flour

<u>Directions</u>
Wash birds well, picking off small feather left on. Mix the salt, pepper and poultry seasoning with flour. Coat bird with flour mixture. Put each bird in the hot oil over medium heat. Cook browning on each side, remove from oil, and drain on paper towels. If gravy is preferred, drain oil from pan, sauté sliced onion set aside. Brown 1 tablespoon of flour in the same pan. Add ¼ cup water. Cook on low heat, stirring constantly scraping the bottom of pan. Place birds in the pan and onions on top of birds. Cover and continue cooking on low turning the birds occasionally. Remove from heat and serve over rice.

Fried Fish

Fish pieces
Salt
Pepper
Oil
Corn meal

Directions
Wash fish. Mix salt, pepper with corn meal. Heat oil and coat fish in meal mixture, place in hot oil. Cook on each side until brown. Remove from oil and drain on paper towels. Cool and enjoy. (If fish pieces are thick, cook longer).

Pan Broil Fish
Fish pieces
Salt
Pepper
2 tablespoons of oil

Directions
Wash fish, drain on paper towels. Place into a greased baking pan. Bake on 350 degrees for 30 minutes or until done. Remove from oven, let cool before serving

Desserts
Sweet Potato Casserole

5 medium sweet potatoes
½ cup sugar (Brown)
¼ cup milk
2 eggs
2 teaspoons cinnamon
¼ cup raisins
1/4cup shredded coconut
4 tablespoons butter

Directions

Wash and boil potatoes until fork tender. Remove from water and remove skins. Blend removing strings. Combine sugar, milk, cinnamon and eggs with potatoes. Whip well in mixing bowl. Add in butter, raisins and coconut and stir. Pour into a buttered baking dish and bake for 1 ½ hours. Cool and enjoy.

Ruth's Easy Bake Peach Cobbler

1 29 oz. can sliced peaches in light syrup
1 Tablespoon fresh lemon juice
1 Box lemon cake mix
½ teaspoon vanilla flavor
1 Stick of butter
½ cup sugar
1 teaspoon cinnamon

Directions

1. Preheat oven to 350 degrees
2. Pour peaches into a 12 to 14 inch dish or pans
3. Cut peaches into bite size pieces, if desired.
4. Stir in lemon juice, flavor, sugar, and cinnamon. Mix well
5. Sprinkle box of mix over mixture, covering completely.
6. Drizzle ½ of melted butter over cake mix
7. Bake for 35 minutes or until brown
8. Remove from oven and sprinkle remaining cake mix over mixture and drizzle remaining butter over cake mix.
9. Bake again until brown.
10. Cool and enjoy.

Puddings

Banana Pudding

4 to 5 Bananas
Box Pudding (vanilla)
Vanilla Wafers Cookies

Directions
Mix box pudding according to direction on box
Cut bananas into small round pieces
In a deep dish layer cookies, bananas, and pudding until bowl is filled.
Cool for several hours before serving.

Bread Pudding

White bread (light bread)
Raisins
Milk
Coconut
Vanilla Flavor
¼ cup brown sugar
1/8 cup of honey

Directions
Soak bread in milk overnight
Combine raisins, coconut, flavor, sugar and honey with milk and bread stir well, stir in a small amount of flour to hold it together. Pour in a baking pan and bake at 350° until done.

French Fried Apples

Firm Apples
Salt
Pepper
Oil

Directions
Wash apples, season with salt and pepper.
Slice apples and fry in a small amount of olive oil.

Coconut Cream Cake

2 cups sifted cake flour
1 ½ cups sugar
½ shortening (Crisco)
1 teaspoon salt
1 Cup milk
3 eggs
Vanilla flour
1 (6 oz.) can froze cream of coconut

Directions

Cream sugar, shortening, egg, salt, flour, ½ cup milk, stir in baking powder. Beat on medium speed for 3 minutes. Add flavor stir well. Bake in 2 9 inch greased and floured cake pans at 375° for 30 minutes. Remove from oven, cool on damp paper towel. Remove from pan, place one layer on cake plate, mix and cream coconut with ¾ can water drizzle over each layer, sprinkle over each layer before putting vanilla icing and coconut over each layer and all around the cake. Cool before cutting.

Blackberry Cobbler

2 cups fresh blackberries
1 ½ cup sugar
2 tablespoons lemon juice
4 tablespoon butter
1 can buttermilk biscuits
2 tablespoons flour or cornstarch
1 teaspoon vanilla flour

Directions

Wash berries, cook in ¼ cup water, adding the flour (cornstarch) dissolved in water to the mixture. Stir constantly for five minutes, while cooking on low heat. Remove from heat, add sugar, butter, lemon juice and flavor stir and mix well. Pour mixture in a deep baking dish. Roll biscuits out on flat, floured surface, place strips of biscuits dough over mixture, bake for 30 minutes on 350°. Remove from heat, cool and serve.

Italian Cream Cake

2 cups sugar
3 eggs
1 cup oil
3 cups flour
1 teaspoon salt
1 teaspoon cinnamon
1 teaspoon soda
1 8 oz. can crushed pineapple
2 cups mashed bananas
1 ½ teaspoon vanilla
1 cup nuts

Frosting
8 oz. pack cream cheese
1 box confession sugar
1 stick butter

Directions
Cream sugar, eggs and oil together, add flour, salt, cinnamon, and soda, mix well.
Add can pineapple, bananas, flavor and nuts mix well. Bake in 2 9 inch round pans for 30 minutes until done. Cool cake then frost. Cream cheese with butter and sugar, mix well and whip for 10 minutes.

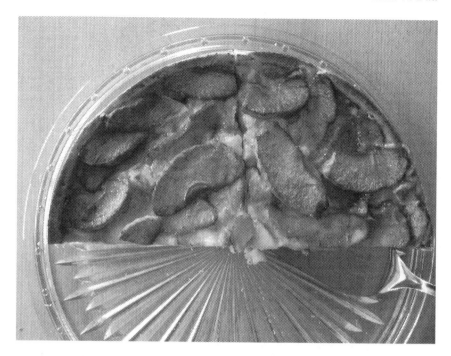

Apple Pie

4 apples   Deep dish pie shell
½ stick butter   1 regular pie shell
½ cup sugar
1 tablespoon cinnamons
1 tablespoon allspice
½ teaspoon vanilla flavor

Directions

Peel and slice apples

Cook in ½ cup water until tender leaving only a very small amount of water in apples. Combine remaining ingredients with apples. Bake pie shell on 350° for 3 to 5 minutes. Remove and pour apple mixture into shell cover mixture with regular pie shell. Bake for 30 minutes with slits into pie shell. The contents should bubble, if not continue cooking until it bubbles and crust is brown.

Peach Pie

1 can of sliced peaches in heavy syrup
½ teaspoon vanilla flavor
½ stick butter
1 tablespoon cinnamon
½ cup sugar
½ tablespoon allspice
1 tablespoon lemon juice
2 deep dish pie crusts

Directions

Cook peaches with syrup over low heat
Combine next six ingredients with peaches.
Cook for 2 minutes more.
Bake one pie shell for 5 minutes.
Pour peach mixture into cooked pie shell.
Cut other shell into long pieces, place over pie in crisscross pattern.
Bake until done and top shell is golden brown.
Brush melted butter over pie before removing from the oven.

Endnotes

1. Notes: Old Eastern Proverb – "If you tell me, I'll forget. If you show me, I may remember. But if you involve me, I'll understand."
2. The Tallahassee Democrat, Tuesday, May 2, 2000 Ross Werland, "Custody Disputes"

Printed in the United States
By Bookmasters